Look What You Can Make With

# Craft Sticks

Edited by Kelly Milner Halls
Photographs by Hank Schneider

## Boyds Mills Press

## Craft Coordinator:
Kelly Milner Halls

## Craft Makers:
Rebecca Ent
Kelly Milner Halls
Kerry O'Neill

## Contributors:

Arlene Macksoud Aissis
Beatrice Bachrach
Katherine Corliss Bartow
Linda Bloomgren
Marie E. Cecchini
Jeanne Corrigan
Clara Flammang
Donna M. Graham
Kelly Milner Halls
Ann E. Hamilton
Edna Harrington

Olive Howie
Helen Jeffries
Tama Kain
Susan Lucci
Carol McCall
June Rose Mobly
Jerry Mundy
Marianne Myers
Joan O'Donnell
Kerry O'Neill
Jane K. Priewe

Bertha W. Reeser
Janet Roelle
Kathy Ross
Dorothea V. Shull
Bernice P. Smith
Cheryl Stees
Sharon Dunn Umnik
Agnes Choate Wonson

Published by Bell Books
Boyds Mills Press, Inc.
A Highlights Company
815 Church Street
Honesdale, Pennsylvania 18431
Printed in China

Publisher Cataloging-in-Publication Data

Look what you can make with craft sticks : over 80 pictured crafts and
dozens of other ideas / edited by Kelly Milner Halls ; photographs by
Hank Schneider.—1st ed.
[48] p. : col. photos. ;  cm.
Includes index.
Summary: Toys, games, and other things to make from craft sticks.
ISBN: 1-56397-997-7
1. Handicraft.  2. Wood crafts.  I. Halls, Kelly Milner.
II. Schneider, Hank.   III. Title.
745.51  21  2001  AC  CIP
2001091965

First edition, 2001
Books in this series originally designed by Lorianne Siomades
The text of this book is set in 10-point Avant Garde Demi, titles 43-point Gill Sans Extra Bold

Visit our Web site at www.boydsmillspress.com

10 9 8 7 6 5 4 3 2 1

# Getting Started

This book is filled with fun, easy-to-make crafts, and each one begins with a craft stick. You'll find a wide variety of things to make, including toys, games, and gifts.

## Directions

Before you start each craft, read the directions and look closely at the photograph, but remember—it's up to you to make the craft your own. If we decorate a craft with markers but you want to use glitter paint and stickers, go for it. Feel free to stray from our directions and invent new crafts.

## Work Area

It's a good idea to keep your work area covered. Old newspapers, brown paper (from grocery bags), or old sheets work well. Also, protect your clothes by wearing a smock. A big old shirt does the job and gives you room to move. Finally, remember to clean up when you've finished.

## Materials

You'll need a lot of craft sticks, so start saving now. Ask friends and relatives to help. Keep your craft-making supplies together, and before making each craft, check the "You Will Need" list to make sure you have everything. You can use either non-toxic acrylic paint or poster paint. A few projects in this book call for tongue depressors. You can find those in craft-supply stores or the craft section of discount department stores. Also, since you'll need scissors, glue, tape, or a stapler for almost every craft, we don't list these supplies.

## Other Stuff

When we show several similar crafts, we'll often list numbered directions that apply to all of the crafts, then specific directions for each craft. Plus, you'll find other ways to jazz up your projects in the "More Ideas" section that appears with every craft. You'll also think of new ideas of your own once you get rolling. So browse through these pages, choose a craft, and have some creative fun. Before you know it, you'll be showing everyone what you made with craft sticks.

# Sail-Away Vessels

"Stick" to this simple plan, and shove off to sea.

## You Will Need:
- plastic foam
- craft sticks and tongue depressors
- yarn and other trims
- paint and paintbrush
- construction paper

## To Make the Rowboat

Cut a triangle shape from plastic foam. Cut tongue depressors to fit each side of the triangle. Glue in place. Break a craft stick in half, and glue each piece to a side of the boat in the back. Lay two craft-stick pieces on top to make seats. Poke a hole in two plastic-foam pieces. Glue to the sides for oarlocks. Add decorative trims.

## To Make the Raft

Apply glue to one side of four craft sticks. Lay them about 1 inch apart. Line twelve craft sticks side by side across the four sticks. Leave enough space between the sixth and seventh sticks to insert one stick. Glue two craft sticks together to form a mast. Glue the mast between the sixth and seventh sticks. Let dry overnight, then paint it and let dry. Cut a piece of construction paper for a sail. Draw a design on it. Cut a tiny slit in the top and bottom of the sail. Thread the sail onto the mast. Add details with decorative trims.

## More Ideas

Glue paper to an empty matchbox to make a storage box for your raft.

Cover your sail with clear self-adhesive paper to protect it.

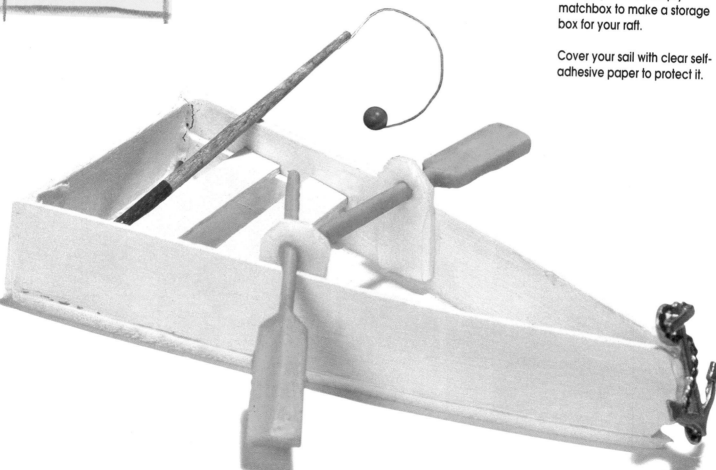

# Stick-to-It Puzzle

Turn your favorite picture into a puzzle.

### You Will Need:
- photograph, old magazine, or poster
- craft sticks

**1** Cut your favorite photo, cartoon, or phrase from a poster or a magazine. (Ask permission first.)

**2** Turn the picture upside down. Cover the back with glue.

**3** Lay your craft sticks touching side to side on the glue side of your picture. Number each stick.

**4** Allow the glue to dry overnight. Ask an adult to cut the sticks apart with a sharp knife to make the puzzle pieces.

## More Ideas
For a real challenge, make a puzzle without numbering the sticks.

Make two puzzles, then give one to a friend. See who can solve the puzzle first.

# Court Jester

This lovable pal will entertain your kingdom.

### You Will Need:
- two craft sticks
- construction paper
- plastic wiggle eye
- cardboard-box scraps
- paint and paintbrush

**1** Glue two craft sticks together to make an X shape.

**2** Cut two construction-paper hearts to form the body. Glue them together with the X sandwiched in between.

**3** Cut a smaller paper heart for the head. Glue a plastic wiggle eye and a paper smile on the face. Add small paper hearts, if you like.

**4** Cut four ½-inch hearts from cardboard-box scraps. Cut small slits into, but not through, the center of the hearts. Paint them, if you wish, and let dry. Press the craft-stick ends into the slits. Glue to secure.

## More Ideas
Can you make a king and queen using the same X base?

# Stick Pals

Make new friends who can come out to play anytime.

## You Will Need:

- craft sticks and tongue depressors
- construction paper
- yarn
- old doll's clothes
- fabric and netting
- embroidery thread
- pompons

## To Make the Girl and Boy

Overlap two crafts sticks to form a leg. Glue two craft-stick legs to the bottom of a single craft-stick body. Add two craft-stick arms just below the other end of the body. Add a paper head, and glue on yarn hair. Dress them in old doll's clothes and shoes.

## To Make the Ballerina

Use a tongue depressor for the body. Add craft-stick arms and legs. Glue on a paper head and yarn hair. Wrap yarn around the body, and glue the ends. Add a fabric-and-netting tutu with a bow of embroidery thread. Add chenille sticks to the legs and pompons to the feet and shoulders.

## More Ideas

Use the craft-stick furniture on pages 8 and 9 to furnish your stick pals' backyard.

# Petite Picnic Set

"Stick" with these instructions to build some outdoor furniture for your pretend playmates.

## You Will Need:

- poster board
- ruler
- craft sticks
- plastic foam
- paint and paintbrush
- four empty thread spools

## To Make the Lounge Chair

Cut a piece of poster board about 6½ inches long by 3 inches wide. Cut craft sticks to fit the width of the poster board, and glue them in place. Cut a second piece of poster board 4 inches long by 3 inches wide. Cut craft sticks 3½ inches long, and glue them to the poster board, leaving a ½-inch tab. Glue the tab underneath the seat. Add glue to the front where the seat and back meet. Glue small pieces of craft sticks to two 3-inch-long pieces of poster board to make arms. Add small pieces of craft sticks underneath, and glue to the seat and back. Add legs.

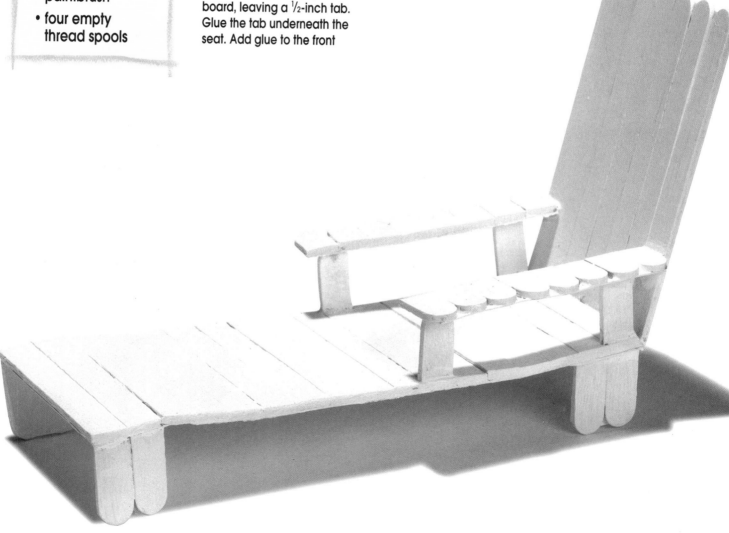

## To Make the Table

Cut a piece of plastic foam
4 inches wide by 6 inches long.
Cover one side with glue, and
apply seventeen craft sticks one
at a time. Break 1 inch off eight
craft sticks. Glue two sticks side
by side, making four pairs, and
let dry. Poke one end of each
leg into the plastic-foam base at
an angle. Glue in place. Glue a
strip of plastic foam where the
legs cross. Paint and let dry.

## To Make the Benches

Cut two pieces of plastic foam
about 1 1/2 inches wide by
4 inches long. Glue four craft
sticks side by side to each piece.
Glue the seat to two thread
spools. Paint and let dry.

## More Ideas

Make an umbrella: Glue a
circle of colorful paper on the
end of a craft stick. Glue the
other end to the center of an
empty thread spool.

# Something Fishy

Net these fantasy fish just for fun.

## You Will Need:

- paint and paintbrush
- craft sticks
- plastic wiggle eye
- yarn

**1** Paint craft sticks in the same or different colors. Let dry. Glue two sticks together at one end, fanning the opposite ends out.

**2** Glue three sticks underneath the top stick and parallel with the bottom stick. Add three dots of glue, 1 inch apart, to the top of those sticks. Place three sticks into the glue, forming a crisscross pattern.

**3** Place one more stick across the entire pattern.

**4** Glue on a plastic wiggle eye. Add yarn for a hanger.

## More Ideas

Make a bed of seaweed. Paint a craft stick green. Curl green chenille sticks around a pencil, then glue one end of each chenille stick to the craft stick. Hang your fish above the seaweed.

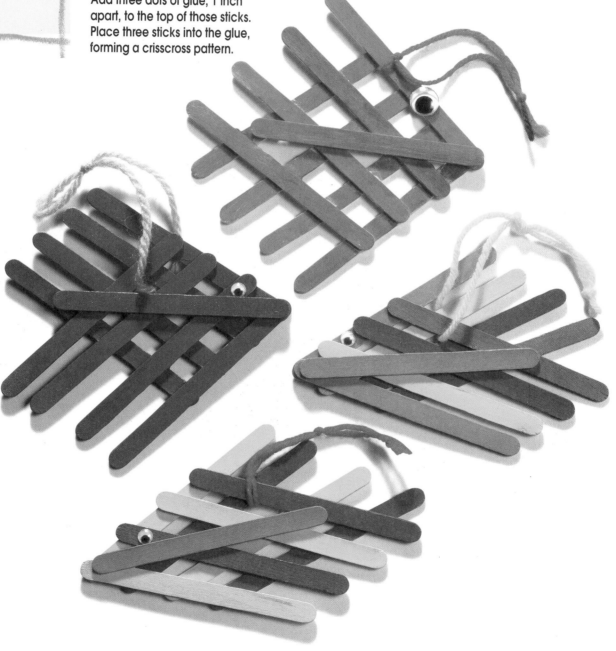

# "Some Bunny Loves You" Card

Send some "bunny" your love with this cheery holiday greeting.

## You Will Need:

- construction paper
- markers
- chenille sticks
- two craft sticks
- small pompon

**1** Fold a piece of construction paper in half. Write a message inside the folded paper.

**2** Cut an oval from a piece of white construction paper, and draw a bunny face.

**3** Cut six small pieces of chenille stick.

**4** Glue the face on the front of the card. Glue craft-stick ears. Glue the chenille-stick pieces on as whiskers and the tiny pompon for the bunny's nose.

## More Ideas

Draw a sun face, and use the craft sticks as the sun's rays.

Glue the tree shape from page 17 to poster board to make a special Christmas card.

# Star-Studded Rainbow

Dazzle your friends with this unusual decoration.

## You Will Need:

- black felt
- eight craft sticks
- rainbow yarn
- craft rhinestones

**1** Cut a 5-inch star shape from black felt.

**2** Tightly wrap each of the eight craft sticks with rainbow yarn, stopping near each end. Tie the yarn in a half-knot and cut the end, leaving a tiny tail.

**3** Glue each yarn-covered stick to the felt star, pointing toward the center of the circle.

**4** Decorate the ends of the sticks with star or other shaped rhinestones. Let dry. Glue a piece of yarn to the back.

## More Ideas

Wrap each craft stick in a different color in "rainbow" order: red, orange, yellow, green, blue, indigo, and violet.

# Picture This

Surround your photos with these unique frames.

## You Will Need:

- craft sticks and tongue depressors
- paint and paintbrush
- photographs
- construction paper
- thin cardboard
- craft rhinestones
- yarn
- poster board
- black marker

### To Make the Triangle-Topped Frame

Place nine craft sticks as shown in the picture. Glue two sticks across them horizontally as shown. Glue one stick vertically over each end stick of the frame. Glue another craft stick over each horizontal stick. For a stand, bend a stick about an inch from its end. Glue the short end to the back. Paint and decorate the frame, and slide a photo through the side.

### To Make the Blackboard Frame

Cut a 4½-by-5-inch piece of black construction paper. Glue craft sticks around it. Add a construction-paper apple and chalk. Glue a photo in the middle. Fold a 5-inch-by-8½-inch piece of cardboard in half. Glue one half to the back of the frame.

## To Make the All-Star Frame

Paint four craft sticks. Let dry. Squeeze glue underneath two craft sticks. Glue them to the top and bottom edges of your photograph. Put a dot of glue on each end of the two craft sticks already in place. Add the last two craft sticks to complete the frame. Decorate with rhinestones, then add a yarn hanger to the back.

## To Make the Harvest Frame

Glue four tongue depressors together. Create two ears of corn from poster board. Add details with a black marker, and glue the corn to the frame. Glue a piece of poster board and a yarn hanger to the back. Glue a photo to the front.

## More Ideas

Don't have star-shaped rhinestones handy? Any decoration will do. Even beans or uncooked popcorn adds color and texture to your picture frame.

# Funny Bunny Hanger

Hop to it! Display this bunny on your doorknob.

## You Will Need:

- five craft sticks
- construction paper
- markers
- thin ribbon

**1** Glue three craft sticks together at the ends to form a square without a top. Glue two craft sticks as crosspieces about 1 inch apart as shown.

**2** Cut a bunny from construction paper. Cut a grassy strip of green construction paper. Cut two small Easter eggs from different-colored paper.

**3** Draw a face on your bunny, and decorate your eggs with markers. Glue the grass strip to the bottom craft stick, then glue the bunny over the grass. Add the eggs.

**4** Glue ribbon to the top fence posts.

## More Ideas

Make a squirrel shape and draw some acorns to add on the fence. Or glue on some small fallen pinecones.

# Easy Easel

Show your favorite photo or artwork with pride.

## You Will Need:

- five craft sticks
- markers
- chenille stick
- sequins, pompons, and other trims

**1** Decorate each craft stick with markers.

**2** Glue two craft sticks with the plain sides together. This will be the easel's tray.

**3** Cut a 2-inch piece of chenille stick. Glue half of the piece to the back of a decorated craft stick near the tip. Let the remaining half stick out.

**4** Glue the last two craft sticks together in a V shape. Let dry.

**5** Glue the edge of the easel tray across the front of the V shape. Let dry. Glue the end of the chenille stick to the point of the V. Let dry. Bend the chenille stick so the easel can stand. Decorate with trims.

## More Ideas

Create an easel twice as big by gluing two craft sticks together at each step.

14

# Plant Projects

Help your greenery grow.

## You Will Need:

- clean empty milk carton
- craft sticks
- construction paper or felt
- potted plant, such as ivy

## To Make the Craft-Stick Trellis

Glue two craft sticks together, end to end, to form one long stick. Center and glue another craft stick across the top of the long stick about 1 inch from the tip. Center and glue another craft stick across the long stick about 1½ inches down from the first. Repeat with a third craft stick about an inch down from the second stick. Glue one craft stick on the left side and one on the right, forming a V shape. Let dry. Stick the trellis into the dirt behind a small ivy plant.

## More Ideas

For a special look, paint the caddy and trellis after the glue has dried, and seal it with clear varnish. Add tiny ribbon flowers.

## To Make the Plant Caddy

Cut away the top half of a clean milk carton so it's a little shorter than the length of a craft stick. Glue craft sticks side by side around the carton. Let dry. Decorate with construction paper or felt. Place a small plant in the caddy.

# Christmas Tree Trims

Decorate for the holidays.

### You Will Need:

- construction paper
- craft sticks
- glitter
- string or yarn
- plastic wiggle eyes
- paint and paintbrush
- sequins or paper stars

### To Make the Glitter Snowflake

Cut a 4-inch-by-4-inch piece of construction paper. Fold the paper in half three times to form a small square. Cut tiny notches out of the edges of the small square, being careful not to cut all of the folds away. Unfold the square to reveal your snowflake. Glue craft sticks around the snowflake to form a frame. Apply a fine layer of glue to the ornament, then add glitter. Let dry, then add a string or yarn hanger.

### To Make Rudolph

Glue two craft sticks together to form a V shape. Glue the third stick across the open end of the V. Cut a red nose from construction paper, and glue it to the bottom of the V. Add two plastic wiggle eyes just under the third stick. Decorate Rudolph's forehead with green paper cut to look like ivy. Add a few red paper berries. Glue ribbon or yarn to Rudolph's ears.

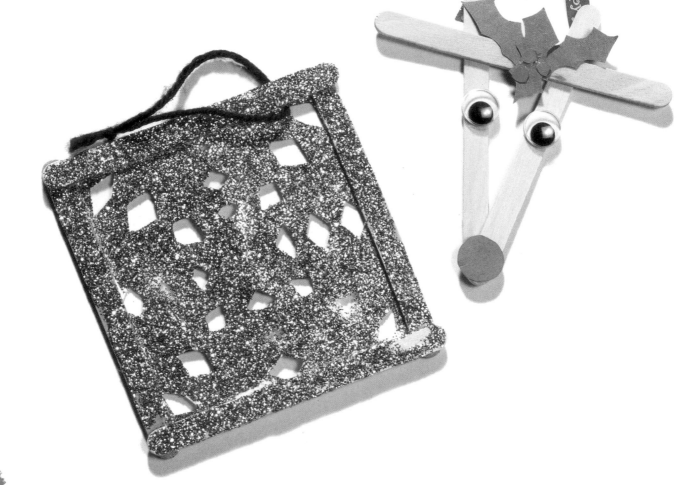

## To Make the Tree Ornament

Paint two sticks brown. Paint seven sticks green. Let dry. Glue the two brown sticks together at one end to form a long tree trunk. Glue the remaining green sticks to form staggered branches. Decorate with sequins or paper stars. Add string or yarn for a hanger.

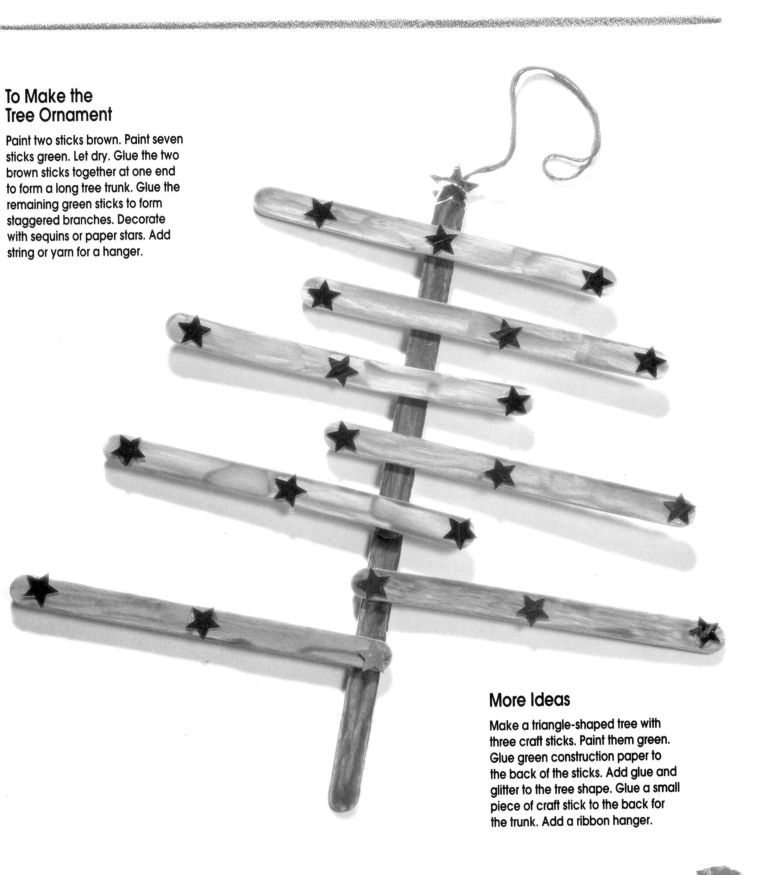

## More Ideas

Make a triangle-shaped tree with three craft sticks. Paint them green. Glue green construction paper to the back of the sticks. Add glue and glitter to the tree shape. Glue a small piece of craft stick to the back for the trunk. Add a ribbon hanger.

# Beautiful Baskets

These craft-stick baskets will come in handy whatever the season.

### You Will Need:

- craft sticks
- plastic-foam tray
- glitter
- plastic berry basket
- cardboard
- poster board

### To Make the Egg Basket

Paint eight craft sticks and let dry. Cut eight egg shapes from a plastic-foam tray. Decorate the eggs with glitter, and let dry. Glue each egg to the end of a craft stick. Let dry. Weave the craft sticks in and out of the sides of a berry basket. Add a dab of glue at each cross point to be sure the sticks stay put.

### To Make the Handle Basket

Cut two squares of cardboard as wide and as tall as a craft stick. Cut tabs 1/4 inch long and the width of a craft stick apart into two sides of each square. Fold back every other tab. Use a dot of glue to attach one end of a craft stick to each folded tab on one square. Glue the other end of each stick to the folded tabs on the other square. Tape a piece of cardboard to fit the bottom. Add a poster-board handle.

### More Ideas

Add seasonal grasses or tissue paper to make this basket a great gift idea. Tuck a small present inside.

18

# Wooden Bracelet

Wrap this around your wrist with pride.

### You Will Need:

- tongue depressor
- bowl of warm water
- clean empty frozen-juice container
- rubber bands
- poster paint and paintbrush
- sequins
- clear nail polish

**1** Soak the wooden tongue depressor in warm water for about an hour, until you can gently bend it around a frozen-juice container. Place rubber bands on top of the tongue depressor to hold it in place. Let dry for one day.

**2** Remove the tongue depressor, cover it with poster paint, and let dry.

**3** Glue on sequins or other trims. Let dry.

**4** Cover with clear nail polish.

### More Ideas

Use this as a headband for a doll.

# Stick-with-a-Heart Bouquet

Express your affection with this pretty heart design.

### You Will Need:

- construction paper
- craft stick
- ribbon

**1** Cut four hearts—two pink and two red—about 2½ inches wide by 2½ inches high.

**2** Cut two 1-inch hearts from green paper. Cut a slightly smaller heart from purple paper.

**3** Arrange the four large hearts to make a heart bouquet at one end of the craft stick, and glue in place. Add the two green hearts to make heart-shaped leaves. Add the small purple heart in the middle of the craft stick.

**4** Add a small ribbon bow. Write a message on the center large heart, if you wish.

### More Ideas

Cut construction-paper tulips or pansies to make a flower bouquet.

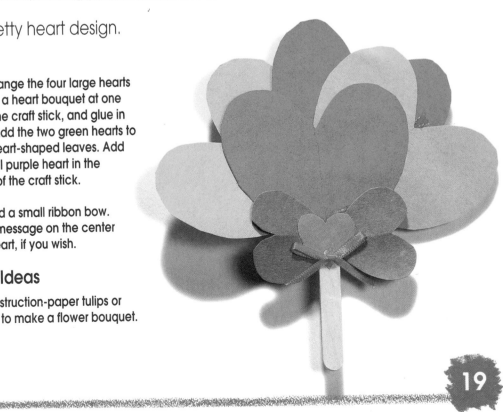

# Fan-tastic Keepsakes

Give one as a Mother's Day gift, or make one for someone special.

## You Will Need:

- poster board or construction paper
- markers
- stickers
- sequins, glitter, and other trims
- craft sticks or tongue depressors
- yarn or ribbon
- coffee filter
- water
- food coloring

## To Make the Personalized Fan

Cut your poster board or construction paper in the fan shape shown. Write a message on the fan. Decorate with stickers, sequins, or other trims. Glue craft sticks or tongue depressors together at the base, then fan them out in the width of your paper fan. Add a fine line of glue to each of the craft sticks. Glue the paper fan on top. Let dry, then add a yarn or ribbon tassel or bow to the base.

## To Make the Rainbow Fan

Color six craft sticks and let dry. Spread the sticks out in a fan shape, and glue the ends together. Spray a coffee filter with water, then color with a few drops of food coloring. Let dry. Fold the filter in half, then in half again. Trim the pointed sections into a curve. Unfold the filter once, then cut the folds at either end to create two sections. Glue a section to each side of the fan. Add sequins and other trims.

## More Ideas

Personalize your fan for that special someone. Is the fan for your teacher? Use apple stickers to dress it up. Is it for your grandmother? She probably loves flowers. Is it for your soccer coach? Soccer-ball stickers should do the trick.

# Greeting Card Stitch-Up

Share your fondest wishes with this special card.

## You Will Need:

- three craft sticks
- hole punch
- old greeting card
- thin ribbon or yarn

**1** Spread glue on one craft stick. Place two craft sticks, side by side, on the first stick.

**2** Punch holes about ½ inch apart around the outside of a closed greeting card.

**3** Put glue on both sides of the top half of the stick handle. Place the glued half of the handle inside the card. Let dry.

**4** Using thin ribbon or yarn, "sew" the front and back of the card together through the punched holes. Start on one side of the stick handle, leaving a 6-inch length of ribbon at the beginning and end. At the last hole, tie the two loose ends of the ribbon together in a bow.

## More Ideas

Stick each card in the bottom of a large plastic-foam cup to make a festive display.

Use the card as a fan.

# Stair-Step Swirl

Stack your sticks into this whirly wonder.

## You Will Need:

- paint and paintbrush
- craft sticks
- thin ribbon

**1** Paint eight sticks in one color, eight sticks in a second color, and eight sticks in a third color—front and back. Let dry.

**2** Select one craft stick of each color. Put a dab of glue at the center of one craft stick. Form an X with the second stick at the glue point. Close the X until the sticks just slightly overlap.

**3** Repeat the process with each of the remaining sticks, making a pattern with your colors.

**4** Before you put the last stick in place, slip a length of ribbon in between the last two sticks. Knot the ribbon, and let dry.

## More Ideas

Make a wider swirl. Glue two sticks together with the tips overlapping. Then arrange a set of these as you would for the smaller swirl.

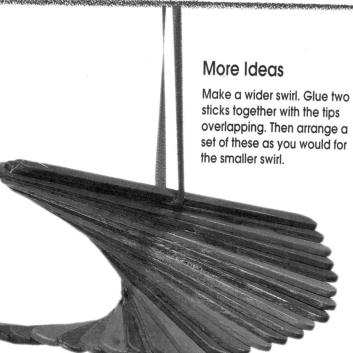

# Bug Magnets

Cheer up your kitchen with these colorful critters.

## You Will Need:

- colored poster board
- paint and paintbrush
- craft sticks
- chenille sticks
- large and small pompons
- plastic wiggle eyes
- magnetic strip

**1** Cut a butterfly, dragonfly, or ladybug shape from poster board.

**2** Paint one craft stick, if you wish, and glue it to the middle of the shape.

**3** Bend a chenille stick into a V, and glue to the end of the craft stick to form the bug's antennae. Add a pompon to make the head.

**4** Add plastic wiggle eyes, if you wish. Decorate the wings. Let dry. Glue a magnetic strip to the back of the craft-stick body.

## More Ideas

Instead of adding a magnet, glue one of your insects to the top of a flat rock to make a paperweight.

# Crafty Desk Set

Set those sticks to hold homework helpers.

## You Will Need:

- craft sticks and tongue depressors
- craft beads or other trims
- clean empty tin cans

### To Make the Notepad Holder

Lay three craft sticks about 1 inch apart, and spread glue on top of each. Center eleven craft sticks side by side on top of the three craft sticks. Place two craft sticks side by side, and glue a third stick on top of the pair. Glue to one end of the craft-stick base. Do the same to the two opposite sides. Lay two tongue depressors as shown, and glue in place. Add beads or other trims.

### To Make the Paper Clip Holder

Break or cut craft sticks to the height of a small can. Glue in place. Add beads or other trims.

### To Make the Pencil Holder

Squeeze a thick line of glue at the top, bottom, and middle of the can, 2 to 3 inches at a time. Place the craft sticks into the glued sections, covering almost all of the can except $1/4$ inch. Cover the gap with a thick line of glue. Add beads or other trims. Let dry.

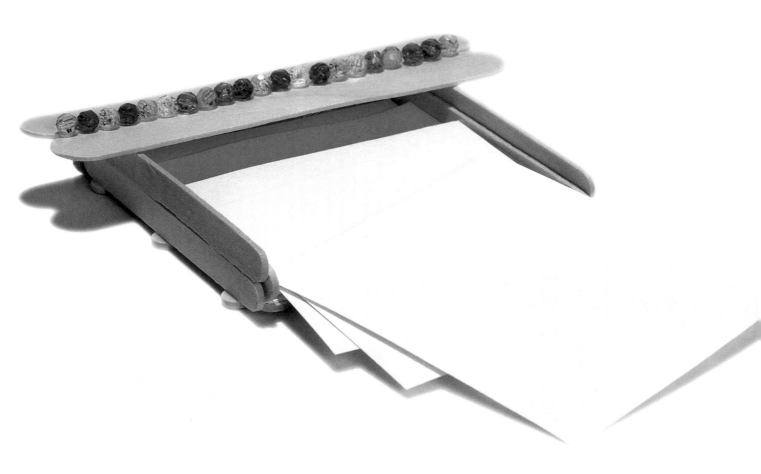

## More Ideas

Paint the craft sticks to match your room color.

Draw a picture on the sticks with markers.

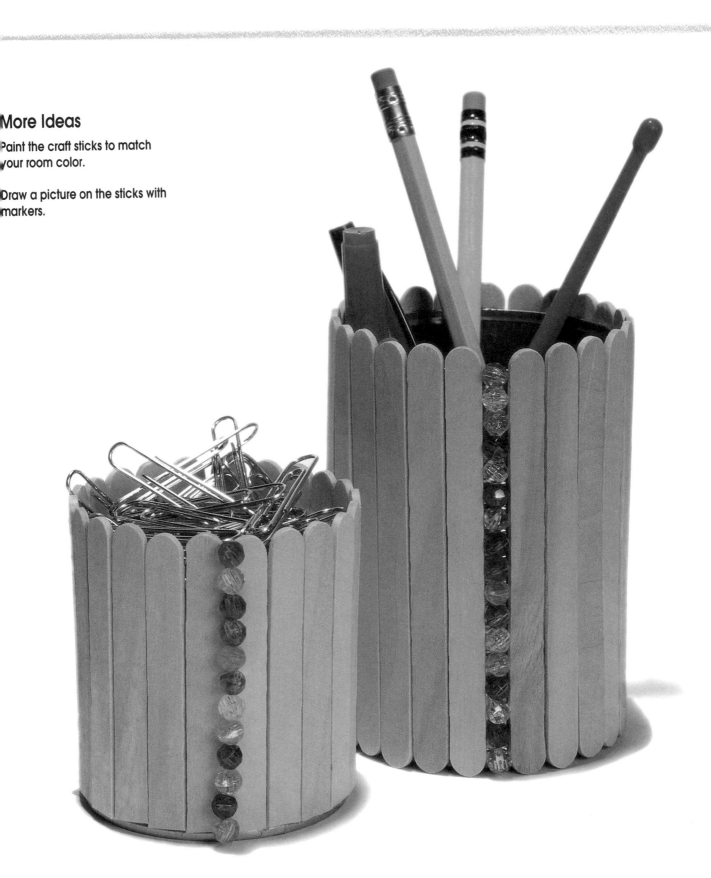

# Easy Stick-Puppet Zoo

This wild and woolly group is easy to tame.

## You Will Need:

- pre-pressed foam animal shapes
- craft sticks

## More Ideas

Cut out the bottom of a shoe box, leaving a 2-inch frame in place to create a puppet theater. Decorate the stage with rain forest drawings or magazine pictures glued to the outside of the box.

You can find foam shapes of every type and style—from sea creatures to dinosaurs to letters of the alphabet—in craft stores. Create life under the sea or a prehistoric land.

**1** Select as many pre-pressed foam shapes as you would like.

**2** Count out as many craft sticks as you have shapes.

**3** Add a spot of glue to the tip of each craft stick. Place the animal shapes on the glue, being careful to keep the tip of the stick in the center of the animal's body.

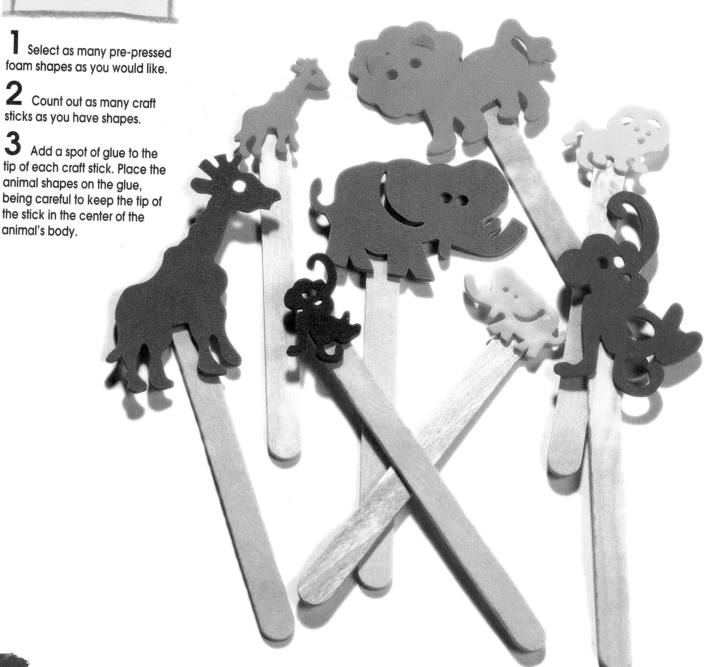

# Craft-Stick Gobbler

Colorful "feathers" make this turkey a hit on Thanksgiving Day.

## You Will Need:

- paint and paintbrush
- 2-inch and 3-inch plastic-foam balls
- craft sticks
- chenille sticks
- felt

**1** Paint the 2-inch plastic-foam ball for the head and let dry. For the body, cut the 3-inch ball in half. Paint one half, and let dry.

**2** Insert about 1 inch of a craft stick into the center of the head. Poke the other end into the body. Wrap a chenille stick around the stick.

**3** Cut a 3-inch piece of chenille stick. Fold it in half, and push the folded end into the face. Add a chenille-stick wattle and felt eyes.

**4** Paint craft sticks, and let dry. Put glue on one end of each stick, and insert the sticks in the body.

## More Ideas

Make a baby turkey using smaller plastic-foam balls and pieces of craft sticks for the feathers.

How about making a peacock? Paint the craft sticks green and blue.

# Spirit Eye

Weave yarn and sticks into something eye-catching in minutes.

## You Will Need:

- two craft sticks
- yarn

**1** Glue two craft sticks together in an X shape.

**2** Beginning at the center of the X, wrap the yarn once around one stick half. Then move to the next and repeat. When you get to the stick half you started with, go around again without overlapping the original yarn loop. Continue in this way. Keep your yarn tight at all times.

**3** When the spaces between the sticks are filled in with yarn, knot the yarn and loop it to form a hanger. Glue to secure.

## More Ideas

Weave several spirit eyes, and give them as gifts.

# Mobiles and Wind Chimes

Use recyclables to make these crafts dance in the breeze.

## You Will Need:

- craft sticks
- metallic chenille sticks
- decorative trims
- embroidery thread
- old compact discs (CDs)
- yarn
- sixteen frozen-juice can lids

## To Make the Juice Jingle Wind Chime

Glue two craft sticks together to form an X. Tie a piece of yarn at the X for a hanger. Cut four 1-foot pieces of yarn. Glue one of the juice-can lids to the end of a piece of yarn, another one almost at the center, and the last one near the top, leaving about 3 inches of yarn. Repeat this three more times. Tie each piece of yarn to one of the sticks. Cut a piece of yarn about 1½ feet long. Glue four lids onto the yarn, leaving about 2½ inches at the top. Tie the yarn to the center of the sticks.

## To Make the Stick and Sparkle Mobile

Wrap six craft sticks in colorful metallic chenille sticks. Add decorative trims, if you wish. Glue a 3½ -inch piece of embroidery thread to one end of each craft stick. Glue the other ends to an old CD. Tie three pieces of embroidery thread together. Knot each loose end, then glue each knot to the center of the CD. Hang the mobile in a sunny place.

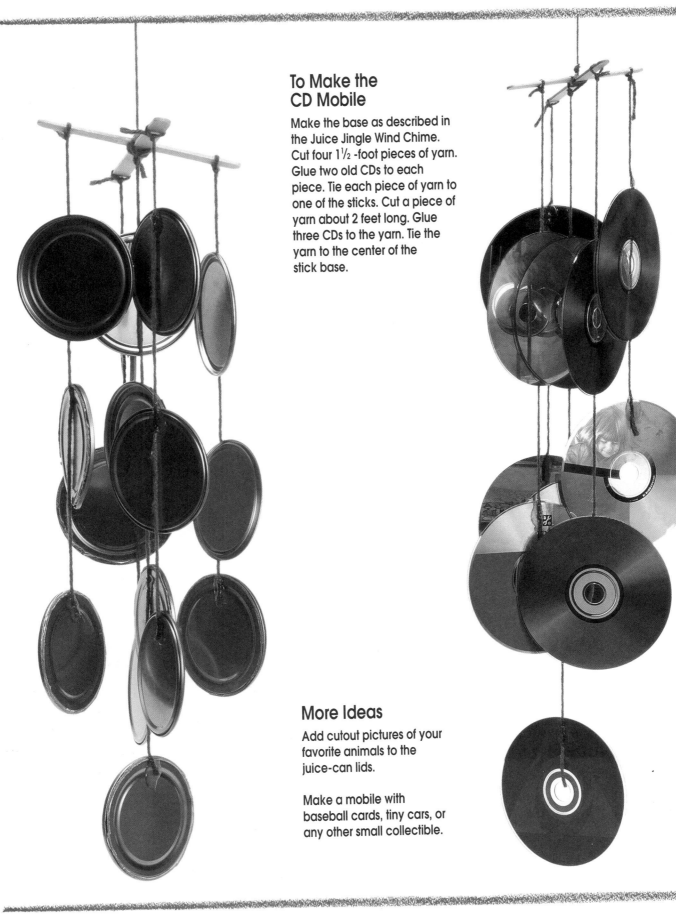

## To Make the CD Mobile

Make the base as described in the Juice Jingle Wind Chime. Cut four 1¹⁄₂ -foot pieces of yarn. Glue two old CDs to each piece. Tie each piece of yarn to one of the sticks. Cut a piece of yarn about 2 feet long. Glue three CDs to the yarn. Tie the yarn to the center of the stick base.

## More Ideas

Add cutout pictures of your favorite animals to the juice-can lids.

Make a mobile with baseball cards, tiny cars, or any other small collectible.

# Flip-and-Match Game

How good is your memory? Try to match these silly sticks and find out.

### You Will Need:

- paint and paintbrush
- twenty craft sticks
- two pairs each of ten different kinds of tiny stickers
- plastic bag

**1** Paint the craft sticks.

**2** Apply one sticker to each stick.

**3** Store the game in a plastic bag.

## How to Play

Place the sticks sticker-side down. Take turns trying to find the matching sticks. Whoever has the most matches at the end of the game wins.

## More Ideas

Add pairs of sticks to the game to make it more challenging.

# Nativity Scene

Create the joy of the Christmas season.

### You Will Need:

- paint and paintbrush
- five craft sticks
- pencil
- construction paper
- old Christmas card
- thin cardboard

**1** Paint five craft sticks, and let dry. Glue them together in a stable shape.

**2** Trace around the stable onto construction paper. Cut out the tracing, and glue it to the back of the stable.

**3** Cut out a Nativity scene from an old Christmas card. Glue it in the stable.

**4** Cut a triangle from thin cardboard. Fold the edges forward, and glue the center to the back of the stable to make it stand up.

## More Ideas

Make the roof of the stable come to a point to make a house, and glue a photo of your family inside.

# Dream Catcher

Hang this near your bed to capture your dreams.

## You Will Need:

- paint and paintbrush
- six craft sticks
- plastic vegetable bag
- thin ribbon
- three craft feathers
- craft rhinestones

**1** Paint each craft stick, front and back, in your favorite color. Let dry.

**2** Glue the sticks to form a hexagon.

**3** Cut a hexagon shape from the vegetable bag, and glue it to the back of the stick hexagon.

**4** Glue three thin ribbons to the hexagon. Glue a feather to one end of each ribbon. Decorate the dream catcher with rhinestones.

**5** Add ribbon to the top for a hanger.

## More Ideas

Make a dream catcher for family members to hang over their beds.

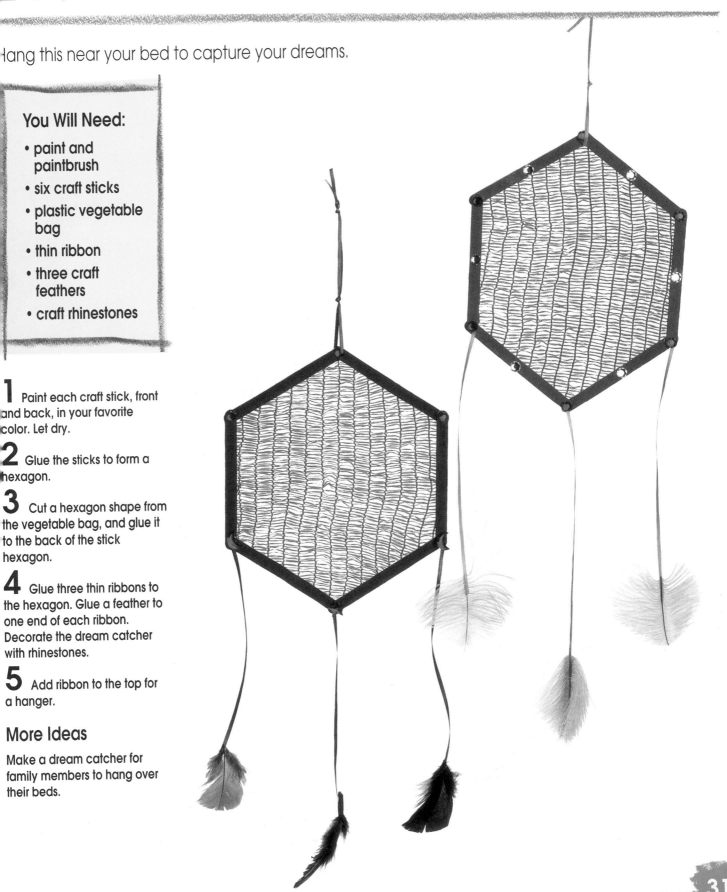

# Craft-Stick Wreaths

Make these wreaths for any season.

**You Will Need:**

- paint and paintbrush
- sixteen craft sticks
- construction paper
- ribbon
- yarn

**3** Glue cut-paper shapes to the wreath.

**4** Add a wide bow at the top. Tie yarn on the back for a hanger.

**1** Paint the crafts sticks, and let dry.

**2** Glue the sticks together in pairs to form X shapes. Arrange the Xs in a wreath shape, and glue them together, end to end.

## More Ideas

Use a cardboard ring as a wreath base. Glue craft sticks around the cardboard. Decorate with paper cutouts.

# Bookmark Buddies

Make these book pals to help you keep your place.

## You Will Need:

- paint and paintbrush
- craft stick or tongue depressor
- markers
- chenille stick
- large or small pompon
- plastic wiggle eyes

**1** Paint the craft stick or tongue depressor. Let dry, then decorate with markers or paint.

**2** Bend a 2-inch piece of chenille stick in half to form a V. Glue the V to one end of the craft stick, pointing up.

**3** Glue on a pompon head and plastic wiggle eyes. Let dry.

## More Ideas

Decorate a potted houseplant with a craft-stick worm poking out of the dirt.

If your pompon head is large enough, you can glue the chenille-stick V to the pompon.

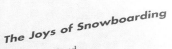

### QUICK REACTION

It's simply my reaction
Who cares
what it's abo[...]
I reach for sa[...]
with my tongue[...]
I stick it out.

### NOT FORGOT

I forgot to take the trash out;
    you didn't tell me that's my job.
I forgot to bring my money;
    you never know when you'll get robbed.
I forgot that game ar[...]

### The Joys of Snowboarding

I laugh out loud
As I float through powder,
Float through the fluffy snow.

I do a front flip
And laugh even louder.
Big air—the way to go!

Down to the lift
Then up again,
Making this board behave

As I speed down the hill
In graceful arcs,
Surfing the winter wave.

### The Snowboarder

Snow, soft, white
In the morning light
Takeoff! And I'm in flight.

Down the hill
In the vivid chill
Bumps, jumps, and nary a spill.

# Ribbon-Weave Trivet

In and out, slow and steady, and you'll create this "hot" gift for your favorite cook.

## You Will Need:

- thirteen craft sticks
- fabric ribbon

**1** Glue four sticks together to form a square frame.

**2** Glue nine sticks side by side on top of the square frame. Leave a small space between each stick. Let dry.

**3** Cut several pieces of ribbon about 10 inches long.

**4** Weave the first ribbon in and out of the sticks. Leave at least 2 inches of ribbon dangling on each side of the square. Weave the second ribbon next to the first, using the opposite pattern. If you went under the first slat with the first ribbon, go OVER the first slat with the second ribbon. Repeat until the trivet is covered.

**5** Glue the loose ends of the ribbons underneath the trivet.

### More Ideas

Use different widths of ribbon to create different designs.

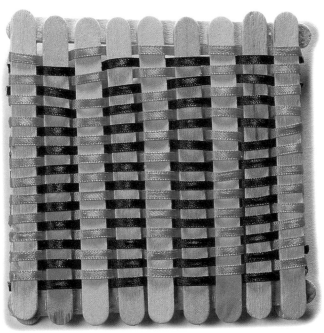

# Teacher's-Pet Remembrance

Tell your favorite teacher you care.

## You Will Need:

- four craft sticks
- stiff black felt
- white gel pen or fabric paint
- red and green construction paper
- ribbon or yarn

**1** Glue four craft sticks together to make a square.

**2** Cut a square of black felt a bit smaller than the craft-stick square.

**3** Write your message on the felt with a white gel pen or white fabric paint. Let dry. Glue the felt square to the back of the craft-stick square.

**4** Cut four apple shapes from red construction paper, and glue to each corner of the frame. Add green leaves.

**5** Glue a ribbon hanger to the back.

### More Ideas

Write your message on paper before you write it on the felt, so you know exactly what you want to say and how you want to write it.

Cut out baseballs or footballs, glue them to the frame, and give it to your dad or grandfather on Father's Day.

# Finger Puppet Frolic

These puppets make it easy to put the finger on fun.

## You Will Need:

- construction paper
- markers
- craft sticks
- plastic wiggle eyes
- chenille sticks, pompons, and other trims

### To Make the Sheep

Cut a sheep shape from construction paper. Draw a face with markers. Break two craft sticks to form two sheep legs and a crosspiece. Color the legs black. Glue the legs to the back of the sheep, and glue the crosspiece just above the legs. Cut a strip of paper, and roll it to form a finger slot. Glue it on the back of the crosspiece. Add a plastic wiggle eye.

### To Make the Frog, Bear, Rabbit, and Penguin

Cut out the animal shapes from construction paper. Add decorative trims. Glue a craft stick vertically to the back. Cut a strip of paper, and roll it to form a finger slot. Glue it on the craft stick.

## More Ideas

Create "habitats" for your animals. Make fences from drinking straws and a heavy-cardboard base for the sheep, a construction-paper pond for the frog, green pompon bushes for the bear, and papier-mâché icebergs for the penguin.

# Stick Tic-tac-toe

Customize your own game of *X*s and *O*s.

**You Will Need:**

- paint and paintbrush
- four craft sticks
- construction paper
- markers
- clear self-adhesive paper
- plastic bag

**1** Paint the craft sticks your favorite color. Let dry.

**2** Lay two sticks parallel about 1½ inches apart. Lay the other two sticks on top of the two parallel sticks to form a crisscross pattern. Glue in place.

**3** Cut ten circles out of construction paper. Mark five with *X*s and five with *O*s.

**4** Cut a 10-inch piece of self-adhesive paper. Cut it in half. Peel the backing off of one piece. Lay the circles on the sticky side. Place the other half of the self-adhesive paper over the top of the circles, sticky side against sticky side.

**5** Cut the circles out of the plastic to form ten game pieces. Store your game in a plastic bag.

## More Ideas

Make a larger grid by overlapping craft sticks at the tips. Lay the grid on a table. Give each box a point value. Toss clean milk caps into the grid. Add up the points.

# Sunflower Place Card

Add some sun to your company dinner table.

**You Will Need:**

- construction paper
- colored pencil or pen
- two tongue depressors
- craft stick

**1** Cut a small piece of construction paper, and write a guest's name on it. Glue it to a tongue depressor.

**2** Glue the other tongue depressor to the first one as shown. Let dry.

**3** Cut a sunflower shape from construction paper.

**4** Paint a craft-stick half green. Glue one end to the back of the sunflower. Glue the other end to the place card.

## More Ideas

Instead of a sunflower, make turkeys for your Thanksgiving Day table.

# Mystery Masks

Shield your identity with these terrific masks.

## You Will Need:

- poster board
- craft sticks
- craft feathers
- craft rhinestones
- glitter
- markers

## To Make the Sparkly Mask

Glue a feather to the front of the mask, being careful not to block the eyehole. Decorate with rhinestones and glitter. Let dry.

## To Make the Totem Pole Mask

Decorate the mask with markers. Add feathers.

## More Ideas

What kind of character would you like to be ? A cat? A dog? A robot? You decide, then use your imagination to decorate your mask.

## To Make the Basic Mask

**1** Cut a mask shape from poster board.

**2** Measure the eyeholes, then cut them out.

**3** Glue a craft stick to the mask on the back. Glue a second craft stick to the end of the first to form a long handle.

# Stick-Puppet Personalities

Use your imagination to create one-of-a-kind characters.

## You Will Need:

- plastic drinking straws
- craft sticks and tongue depressors
- markers
- felt
- straw
- construction paper
- colored pencils
- yarn

### To Make the Scarecrow

Cut three plastic drinking straws in half. Glue three pieces to a tongue depressor vertically for the body and three horizontally for the arms. Draw a face on felt, and glue in place. Fold a piece of felt in half, and cut out a coat shape. Cut a slit in the fold, and slip the coat over the head. Glue in place, and stuff pieces of straw at the hands and feet. Add details.

### To Make the King and Queen

Glue two tongue depressors together to make the body. Add construction-paper clothing to the front and back. Glue pieces of craft sticks for hands. Add a head and crown to the front and back. Draw faces with colored pencil. Glue on yarn hair.

### More Ideas

Make a castle from cardboard tubes.

Make a farm field from three or four plastic-foam trays stacked and glued together. Paint the top brown. Add rows of green chenille-stick "crops." Stick your scarecrow in the field.

Stick-Puppet Personalities

# Star Banners

Let your colors proudly wave with this star decoration.

## You Will Need:

- paint and paintbrush
- four craft sticks
- tissue paper or poster board
- eight craft rhinestones or construction paper
- yarn or ribbon

## More Ideas

Make these banners your own. Decorate them with glitter, stickers, beads—it's up to you.

**1** Paint four craft sticks in the same or different colors.

**2** Glue the sticks together to form an eight-pointed star.

**3** Add tissue-paper or poster-board streamers to the lower half of the star points. Glue a rhinestone or a paper star on the end of each point.

**4** Add a yarn or ribbon hanger.

# Pressed-Flower Window Wonder

Capture the colors of spring all year long.

### You Will Need:

- white paper
- small wild flowers
- heavy book
- clear self-adhesive paper
- eight craft sticks
- ribbon or yarn

**1** Fold a sheet of plain white paper. Place brightly colored wild flowers inside the folded paper. Put the paper between the pages of a heavy book. (It will take about ten days for the flowers to dry.)

**2** Arrange the dried flowers on the sticky side of a 5-inch-by-5-inch piece of clear self-adhesive paper. Place another 5-inch piece of self-adhesive paper on top of the first.

**3** Glue four craft sticks together to make a square. Let dry.

**4** Glue the flower square to the craft-stick square. Glue four more craft sticks on top of the square.

**5** Add a ribbon hanger to the back.

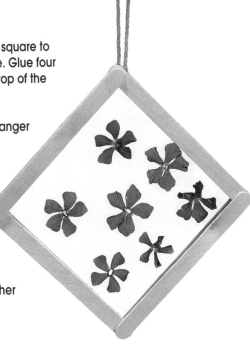

### More Ideas

Instead of a square window, make another shape to hold your flowers.

# Mirror, Mirror on the Doll

Get a grip on this smiling face—and your own.

### You Will Need:

- construction paper
- poster board
- aluminum foil
- craft stick
- markers
- yarn or synthetic hair

**1** Cut construction paper and poster board into an oval shape exactly the same size—about 2½ inches wide by 3½ inches long.

**2** Cover the poster-board oval with aluminum foil on one side. Wrap the foil to the back of the oval.

**3** Glue the craft stick to the back of the "mirror" so that most of it sticks out at the bottom.

**4** Draw a silly face on one side of the construction-paper oval. Glue the face to the back of the "mirror" so the craft stick handle is sandwiched in between.

**5** Add yarn or synthetic hair to the paper face. Decorate the mirror handle.

### More Ideas

Make your mirror into a clown face. Or how about a cat? Just vary the colors and shapes of your mirror.

# Wood Plaques

Make these decorative panels for any occasion.

## You Will Need:

- craft sticks
- old magazine or catalog
- yarn
- construction paper
- markers
- red, white, and blue sticker stars or sequins
- chenille stick

### To Make the Basic Plaque

**1** Apply glue on the back of two craft sticks. Lay them about 3 inches apart.

**2** Place about ten craft sticks side by side across the two sticks, with no spaces showing. Let dry.

### To Make the Cow Plaque

Cut out your favorite cow picture from a magazine or a catalog. Glue it to the plaque. Add a yarn hanger.

### To Make the Election Day Plaque

Write "vote" in big, bold letters across a piece of white construction paper, using red and blue markers. Outline the letters in black, if you like. Glue the paper to the front of the plaque. Decorate the ends of the sticks with red, white, and blue sticker stars or sequins. Add other trims. Let dry. Glue a chenille stick bent into a V shape to the back of the sign as a hanger.

## More Ideas

Make a nameplate for your room, and hang it on the doorknob.

# Star of David Garland

Make the Hanukkah or Passover holiday even more festive.

**You Will Need:**

- crafts sticks
- glitter
- embroidery thread

**1** Make Star of David shapes from craft sticks.

**2** Add glue and glitter on each star.

**3** Tie them together with embroidery thread. Add thread at each end to hang.

### More Ideas

Arrange the stars in a circle to create a sparkly centerpiece for your holiday table.

# Personal Magnet Banner

Show the world what you like best.

**You Will Need:**

- craft sticks
- old magazines or catalogs
- stickers or other trims
- magnetic strip

**2** Cut letters from an old magazine or catalog to spell out your name or the name of the person you want to describe. Glue the letters in place. Add stickers or other trims.

**3** From the same magazine, cut out three tiny pictures that you like or that remind you of the person named on the banner.

**4** Glue the pictures to the sticks. Glue a magnetic strip to the back.

### More Ideas

Create a Personal Magnet Banner as big as the plaque on page 44. Add your favorite pictures.

**1** Cover three craft sticks with glue, and lay them side by side. Lay four craft sticks side by side over the glued sticks. (Half of each stick will be in contact with the glued sticks.)

# Sled Ornament

Remember good times with this winter decoration.

**You Will Need:**

- six craft sticks
- felt and other trims
- glitter markers or paint and paintbrush
- ribbon

Line up five sticks side by side as shown in the picture.

Spread glue across the back of the remaining stick. Place it across the five sticks about 1 inch from the tip of the center stick. Let dry.

Decorate your sled with felt or other trims. Write your name or the name of a friend or family member on the center stick. Use glitter markers, or paint the sticks in your favorite color.

Add a ribbon hanger.

## More Ideas

Add runners by stacking and gluing three sticks underneath the sled on both sides.

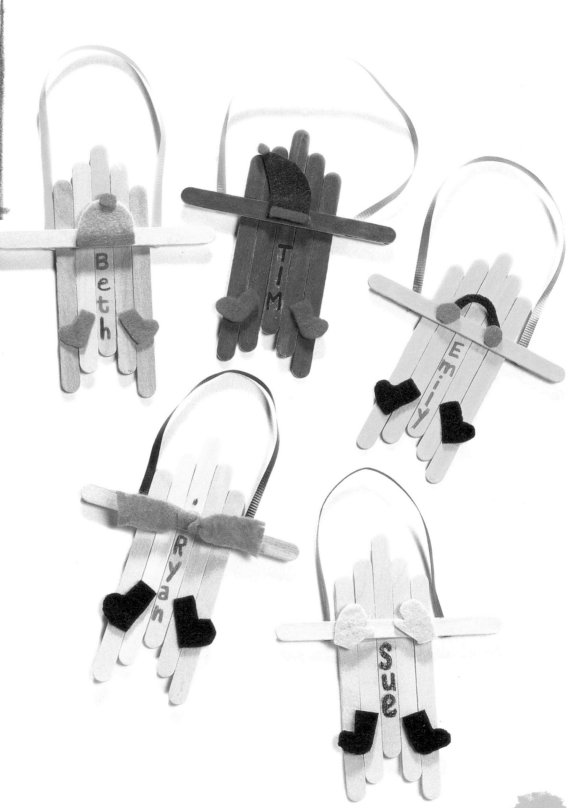

# Title Index

Beautiful Baskets . . . . . . . . . . 18
Bookmark Buddies . . . . . . . . . 34
Bug Magnets . . . . . . . . . . . . . 23
Christmas Tree Trims . . . . . . . 16
Court Jester . . . . . . . . . . . . . . 6
Craft-Stick Gobbler . . . . . . . . 27
Craft-Stick Wreaths . . . . . . . . 32
Crafty Desk Set . . . . . . . . . . . 24
Dream Catcher . . . . . . . . . . . 31
Easy Easel . . . . . . . . . . . . . . 14
Easy Stick-Puppet Zoo . . . . . . 26
Fan-tastic Keepsakes . . . . . . . 20

Finger Puppet Frolic . . . . . . . . 36
Flip-and-Match Game . . . . . . 30
Funny Bunny Hanger . . . . . . . 14
Greeting Card Stitch-Up . . . . . 22
Mirror, Mirror on the Doll . . . 43
Mobiles and Wind Chimes . . 28
Mystery Masks . . . . . . . . . . . 39
Nativity Scene . . . . . . . . . . . 30
Personal Magnet Banner . . . 46
Petite Picnic Set . . . . . . . . . . 8
Picture This . . . . . . . . . . . . . 12
Plant Projects . . . . . . . . . . . . 15

Pressed-Flower
  Window Wonder . . . . . . . . . . 43
Ribbon-Weave Trivet . . . . . . . 35
Sail-Away Vessels . . . . . . . . . . 4
Sled Ornament . . . . . . . . . . . 47
"Some Bunny Loves You" Card . 11
Something Fishy . . . . . . . . . . . 10
Spirit Eye . . . . . . . . . . . . . . . . 27
Stair-Step Swirl . . . . . . . . . . . 22
Star Banners . . . . . . . . . . . . . 42
Star of David Garland . . . . . . 46
Star-Studded Rainbow . . . . . . 11

Stick Pals . . . . . . . . . . . . . . . .
Stick-Puppet Personalities . . .
Stick Tic-tac-toe . . . . . . . . . . .
Stick-to-It Puzzle . . . . . . . . . .
Stick-with-a-Heart Bouquet . .
Sunflower Place Card . . . . . . .
Teacher's-Pet Remembrance
Wood Plaques . . . . . . . . . . . .
Wooden Bracelet . . . . . . . . . .

# Subject Index

## ANIMALS
bear finger puppet . . . . . . . . 36
Bookmark Buddies . . . . . . . . . 34
Bug Magnets . . . . . . . . . . . . . 23
Craft-Stick Gobbler . . . . . . . . 27
Easy Stick-Puppet Zoo . . . . . . 26
Finger Puppet Frolic . . . . . 36, 37
frog finger puppet . . . . . . . . . 36
penguin finger puppet . . . . . . 36
rabbit finger puppet . . . . . . . 36
Rudolph the reindeer . . . . . . . 16
sheep finger puppet . . . . . . . 36
Something Fishy . . . . . . . . . . . 10

## BASKETS
Beautiful Baskets . . . . . . . . . . 18
egg basket . . . . . . . . . . . . . . . 18
handle basket . . . . . . . . . . . . 18

## DESK ACCESSORIES
all-star frame . . . . . . . . . . . . 13
blackboard frame . . . . . . . . . 12
Crafty Desk Set . . . . . . . 24, 25
Easy Easel . . . . . . . . . . . . . . 14
harvest frame . . . . . . . . . . . . 13
notepad holder . . . . . . . . . . . 24
paper clip holder . . . . . . . . . . 24
pencil holder . . . . . . . . . . . . . 24
Picture This . . . . . . . . . . . 12, 13
triangle-topped frame . . . . . . 12

## GAMES
Flip-and-Match Game . . . . . . 30
Stick Tic-tac-toe . . . . . . . . . . . 38

## GIFTS
all-star frame . . . . . . . . . . . . 13
Beautiful Baskets . . . . . . . . . . 18

blackboard frame . . . . . . . . . 12
craft-stick trellis . . . . . . . . . . . 15
Dream Catcher . . . . . . . . . . . 31
Easy Easel . . . . . . . . . . . . . . 14
egg basket . . . . . . . . . . . . . . . 18
Fan-tastic Keepsakes . . . 20, 21
Greeting Card Stitch-Up . . . . . 22
handle basket . . . . . . . . . . . . 18
harvest frame . . . . . . . . . . . . 13
Personal Magnet Banner . . . 46
personalized fan . . . . . . . . . . 20
Picture This . . . . . . . . . . . 12, 13
plant caddy . . . . . . . . . . . . . . 15
Plant Projects . . . . . . . . . . . . 15
Pressed-Flower
  Window Wonder . . . . . . . . . . 43
rainbow fan . . . . . . . . . . . . . . 20
Ribbon-Weave Trivet . . . . . . . 35
Sled Ornament . . . . . . . . . . . 47
"Some Bunny Loves You" Card . 11
Spirit Eye . . . . . . . . . . . . . . . . 27
Stair-Step Swirl . . . . . . . . . . . 22
Star-Studded Rainbow . . . . . . 11
Stick-with-a-Heart Bouquet . . 19
Teacher's-Pet Remembrance 35
triangle-topped frame . . . . . . 12

## HOLIDAY AND OTHER
  DECORATIONS
Beautiful Baskets . . . . . . . . . . 18
Bug Magnets . . . . . . . . . . . . . 23
Christmas Tree Trims . . . . . 16, 17
CD mobile . . . . . . . . . . . . . . . 29
Court Jester . . . . . . . . . . . . . . 6
cow plaque . . . . . . . . . . . . . . 44
Craft-Stick Gobbler . . . . . . . . 27
Craft-Stick Wreaths . . . . . . 32, 33
Dream Catcher . . . . . . . . . . . 31

egg basket . . . . . . . . . . . . . . . 18
Election Day plaque . . . . . . . 44
Fan-tastic Keepsakes . . . 20, 21
Funny Bunny Hanger . . . . . . . 14
glitter snowflake . . . . . . . . . . 16
Greeting Card Stitch-Up . . . . . 22
handle basket . . . . . . . . . . . . 18
juice jingle wind chime . . . . 28
Mobiles and Wind Chimes . . 28, 29
Nativity Scene . . . . . . . . . . . 30
Personal Magnet Banner . . . 46
personalized fan . . . . . . . . . . 20
Pressed-Flower
  Window Wonder . . . . . . . . . . 43
rainbow fan . . . . . . . . . . . . . . 20
Ribbon-Weave Trivet . . . . . . . 35
Rudolph the reindeer . . . . . . . 16
Sled Ornament . . . . . . . . . . . 47
Something Fishy . . . . . . . . . . . 10
Spirit Eye . . . . . . . . . . . . . . . . 27
Stair-Step Swirl . . . . . . . . . . . 22
Star Banners . . . . . . . . . . . . . 42
Star of David Garland . . . . . . 46
Star-Studded Rainbow . . . . . . 11
stick and sparkle mobile . . . . 28
Stick-with-a-Heart Bouquet . . 19
Sunflower Place Card . . . . . . . 38
tree ornament . . . . . . . . . . . . 17
Wood Plaques . . . . . . . . . 44, 45

## PLANT CONTAINERS
  AND ACCESSORIES
craft-stick trellis . . . . . . . . . . . 15
plant caddy . . . . . . . . . . . . . . 15
Plant Projects . . . . . . . . . . . . 15

## THINGS TO WEAR
Wooden Bracelet . . . . . . . . . . 19

## TOYS
ballerina stick pal . . . . . . . . .
bear finger puppet . . . . . . . .
boy stick pal . . . . . . . . . . . . .
Easy Stick-Puppet Zoo . . . . . .
Finger Puppet Frolic . . . . . . 36,
frog finger puppet . . . . . . . . .
girl stick pal . . . . . . . . . . . . . .
king puppet . . . . . . . . . . . . . .
lounge chair . . . . . . . . . . . . . .
Mirror, Mirror on the Doll . . . .
Mystery Masks . . . . . . . . . . . .
penguin finger puppet . . . . . .
Petite Picnic Set . . . . . . . . . . 8
picnic table and benches . . .
queen puppet . . . . . . . . . . . .
rabbit finger puppet . . . . . . .
raft . . . . . . . . . . . . . . . . . . . . .
rowboat . . . . . . . . . . . . . . . . .
Sail-Away Vessels . . . . . . . . . . 4
scarecrow puppet . . . . . . . . .
sheep finger puppet . . . . . . .
sparkly mask . . . . . . . . . . . . .
Stick Pals . . . . . . . . . . . . . . . .
Stick-Puppet Personalities . . 40,
Stick-to-It Puzzle . . . . . . . . . .
totem pole mask . . . . . . . . . .

## VESSELS
raft . . . . . . . . . . . . . . . . . . . . .
rowboat . . . . . . . . . . . . . . . . .
Sail-Away Vessels . . . . . . . . . 4,